Introdu

The **Wye** must be a bilingual river
rising high on the slopes of Pu
Severn's birthplace. It tumbles thr
lowlands of Herefordshire. But its lower re
sandstone and limestone hills to form a spectacular gorge of exceptional
beauty. In these last miles the Wye returns to mark the border before being
reunited with its erstwhile sibling just below Chepstow.

The Lower Wye Valley is cherished for its dramatic and captivating
landscapes, turbulent history and varied wildlife. The area has drawn visitors
since the dawn of tourism, among its more famous suitors the ubiquitous
Wordsworth and Turner. Ten walks explore these lower reaches of the Wye
valley. Despite its renown, you will find plenty of quiet glades and tranquil
viewpoints.

The Forest of Dean spreads across a wedge of elevated ground between the
Wye and Severn. It was established as a royal hunting forest in 1066, though
there are remains from Bronze and Iron ages and traces of Roman occupation.
In more recent centuries, timber, charcoal, iron and coal production have
been the mainstay of the Dean's livelihood. This has bequeathed an intriguing
blend of industrial history and great natural beauty. The Royal Forest of
Dean has always been a place of spirited independence. Strictly speaking it
encompasses just the wooded areas between Lydbrook, Parkend, Coleford and
Cinderford. Native born foresters still have rights of pasture and prospecting.

This is border country where Wales and England are both divided and
fused. The old bridge at Redbrook once carried the Wye Valley Railway across
the river's swirling waters and the border itself. The footbridge now clamped
to its side (**Walk 7**) epitomises the relationship between these two diverse but
closely connected regions. To the east rises the great plateau of Dean, to the
west the hills of Gwent.

You will encounter human attempts to harness and develop the great
natural resources of 'Wyedean': coal and iron in the Forest (**Walk 14**); railways
and tram roads (**Walk 15**); water and wire at Tintern (**Walk 2**). There is much
history to enrich magnificent walking: a Cistercian Abbey at Tintern (**Walk 1**);
a Georgian dining house at the Kymin (**Walk 8**); a medieval castle at Goodrich
(**Walk 10**); a megalithic standing stone at Staunton (**Walk 11**); and the line
of the eighth century Offa's Dyke (**Walk 3**). But above all the splendour and
variety of forest, heath, hills and gorges makes this a superlative walking area.

This is a great area to explore, with much to see on wet days as well as fine
ones.

Enjoy it!

TINTERN & BROCKWEIR

DESCRIPTION A short, enjoyable 3-mile circumnavigation around the heart of the Wye gorge. The outward route hugs the steep wooded English slopes, while the return path meanders through waterside meadows. The attractive village of Brockweir and the countryside centre at Tintern Old Station provide plenty of interest.
START Tintern Abbey car park. SO 533001
DIRECTIONS Tintern is on the A466 between Monmouth and Chepstow.
PUBLIC TRANSPORT Bus 69 travels between Chepstow and Monmouth daily, including Sundays. There are stops at both Tintern and Brockweir.

Tintern Abbey is the best-preserved medieval abbey in Wales. Founded in 1131 by Cistercian monks, it escaped the worst of medieval instability through being tucked away from the more contentious regions of Wales. It did not, however, escape the dissolution of the monasteries by Henry VIII in 1536. It's not so much the exemplary Gothic architecture, as its natural amphitheatre that gives Tintern evocative charm. Here is one of Wales' original tourist attractions. Wordsworth wrote a poem about it, Turner painted it. According to an undated legend, a group of young men decided to excavate the precincts one day. They discovered the remains of two bodies and celebrated their find with open-air revels. During the evening a thunderstorm interrupted the proceedings and the youths were horrified to see the figure of a knight clad in armour surrounded by the ghostly spectre of hooded monks. Apparently they had disturbed the rest of the Earl of Pembroke, known as 'Strongbow'. As the knight appeared to raise his sword, the young men fled in instant sobriety. Tintern is now in the care of Cadw and is well worth a visit. Entrance charge.

I From the abbey car park, follow the riverside path upstream with the Wye on your right. This leads past some houses and soon arrives on to the main road. Continue along the main road past the Abbey Mill. Then TURN RIGHT and cross the footbridge over the river. This served Tintern wire works, branching off the Wye Valley railway, which ran under the hill opposite. As you cross the water, you also pass from Wales into England. On the far side continue along the track *and enjoy views back across the river.* At a signpost for 'Devil's Pulpit', TURN LEFT to follow a stony path slanting up the side of the hill past some metal bollards. There is a steep climb between holly bushes but soon you gain the narrow ridge that has forced the Wye into a tight loop around the hill.

2 At a path junction by a stone wall, KEEP STRAIGHT AHEAD ignoring the right hand branch climbing to the Devil's Pulpit. (This is **Walk 3**). The broad path gradually descends with views across to the Welsh bank. After ¾ mile you reach the village of Brockweir and soon come to the Brockweir Inn at a junction of lanes. A short walk up the hill to the right brings you to Brockweir Village Shop; *a community venture specialising in local produce and also offering a coffee shop.* At the pub, BEAR LEFT and cross the bridge back into Wales.

3 At the far side of the bridge, just before you reach the main road, TURN LEFT and follow a footpath sign to Tintern. Climb down the steps and continue ahead following the course of the dismantled railway. (If you prefer, you can follow the riverside path to the left.)

4 You soon reach Tintern Old Station. *The station is now a countryside centre run by Monmouthshire County Council. This is a good place to explore. There is a café, shop, exhibition and video room. Posters demonstrate the wide variety of excursions that ran here from the South Wales valleys in the days when steam trains ploughed up and down the line. Now the meadows are managed for wild flower conservation. At the far end of the station are the Old Station Sculptures, a series of six carved wooden sculptures repre-*

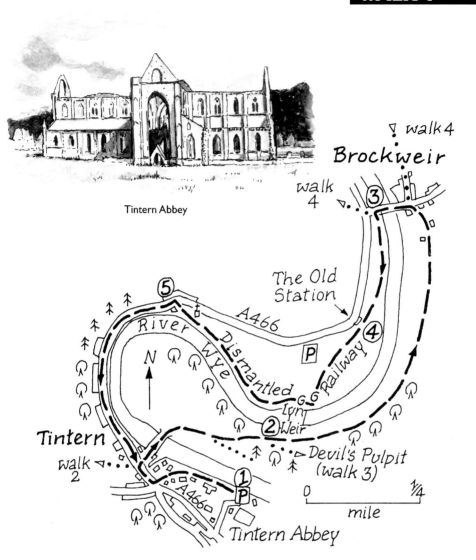

Tintern Abbey

senting historical and mythical figures from the medieval borderlands. There is pay and display parking at the Old Station so you can begin and end the walk here if you wish.

From the Old Station, FOLLOW THE TRACK OF THE DISMANTLED RAILWAY, also a working miniature railway for the first part! The track bed ends abruptly at the river, as there is no crossing now. At this point, TURN RIGHT down some steps off the embankment to reach the riverside path below. TURN RIGHT through a gate and follow the path through the riverside meadows. Pass through the churchyard next to St Michael's Church and then along a narrow lane to reach the main road.

5 TURN LEFT and follow the main road back to the abbey. *The grand scenery is compensation for the traffic.*

TINTERN & THE ANGIDY VALLEY

DESCRIPTION Once, the steep valley sides echoed with the clamour of iron production. Now it is birdsong that resonates through the attractive woodland in the Angidy valley. This 3½ mile exploration of the Wye's fast flowing tributary investigates industrial and natural history on the Welsh border.

START Tintern Abbey car park. SO 533001. For information about the abbey, see **Walk 1**.

DIRECTIONS Tintern is on the A466 between Monmouth and Chepstow.

PUBLIC TRANSPORT Bus 69 Chepstow – Tintern – Monmouth, daily, including Sundays.

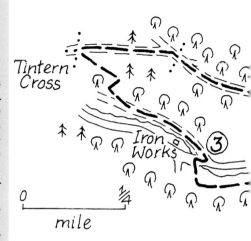

I From the abbey car park, follow the riverside path upstream with the Wye on your right. This leads past some houses and soon arrives on to the main road. Continue along the main road past the Abbey Mill. Opposite the entrance to the Abbey Mill car park, TURN LEFT up a steep tarmac lane. After a few yards, TURN SHARP LEFT to follow a footpath sign 'Tintern Trail'. The route climbs through the woods in a sunken lane between walls up towards Barbadoes Woods. After a while, the path levels out and then follows a terrace above the Angidy valley. You pass a left hand turning for the Tintern Trail. You ignore this (although you could use it as short cut to near point 4 if you wanted to reduce the length of the walk.) Shortly after this turning you rise up to join a forestry road. BEAR LEFT along it and immediately afterwards come to a major junction.

2 Carry STRAIGHT ON, curving gently up to the left on the forestry road. This climbs steadily for nearly ½ mile before coming to another junction. At this point, BEAR LEFT past a barrier and follow the track gently down hill. You now need to WATCH OUT carefully for the next turning. About 300 yards past the junction the track is crossed by a public footpath, but it is not obvious unless you keep your eyes open. The branch to the

right is marked by a yellow arrow as it climbs up hill. Our route is almost opposite this SHARP LEFT. There is no sign or waymarker but it is a clear path leading diagonally back down the hillside. Follow this as it zig-zags down to the valley floor where it meets a track. TURN LEFT and follow this track to the road. Just to the right lies the old furnace.

A bbey Tintern Furnace was a blast furnace which smelted iron using charcoal as a fuel. Its cast iron was made into utensils or passed to the other forges in the valley to be wrought, reducing the carbon content and making it more useful. This wrought iron was made into wires by the Tintern wire works. The furnace closed in the seventeenth century. The remains are now in the care of Monmouthshire County Council and the site is open to visitors, free of charge.

3 Return to the road and just before the bridge TURN RIGHT (south) following a sign to Glyn Wood and Tintern. The path lies beside the brook, crosses a wooden footbridge and then passes to the right of a millpond used for fishing. At the far side of this water, take the RIGHT HAND FORK which climbs diagonally into the woods. Ignore any cross tracks or turnings. When you come to a road, TURN LEFT and follow this down hill for about 200 yards.

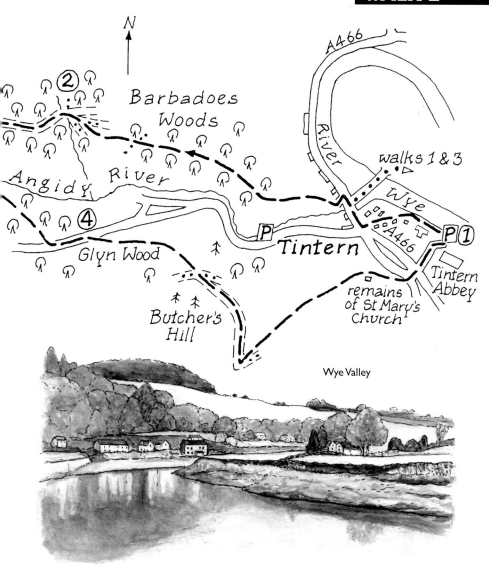

Wye Valley

4 Then leave the road to BEAR RIGHT along a bridleway signposted to Butcher's Hill and Church Grove. Continue along this forest road, ignoring another track crossing it. At the top (Butcher's Hill) the track sweeps left around the head of a small valley. As you round the curve, BEAR LEFT at a fork and descend the main track passing Grove House. After the house continue ahead on a foot-path heading down through the trees, now with views across the Wye Valley. Just above Tintern you pass the remains of St Mary's Church. This was destroyed by fire in 1977. Beyond the church continue to follow the path, which is cobbled and could be slippery. Then take some rough stone steps to return to the main road opposite the abbey.

TINTERN, OFFA'S DYKE & THE DEVIL'S PULPIT

DESCRIPTION History and great natural beauty endow Tintern with a unique charm. A climb through craggy woodland brings you to the impressive remains of Offa's Dyke, guarding the ancient border between Mercia and Wales. Through the trees enjoy the classic view of the historic abbey ruins set in a loop of the Wye. The return route descends down to the valley and follows the course of the railway track back to Tintern, a total of 5½ miles.

START Tintern Abbey car park. SO 533001

DIRECTIONS Tintern is on the A466 between Monmouth and Chepstow.

PUBLIC TRANSPORT Bus 69 travels between Chepstow and Monmouth via Tintern, daily including Sundays.

T intern is now the epitome of tranquillity, wooded hillsides embracing the picturesque waters of the Wye, which entwines itself around the photogenic ruins of the Cistercian abbey. It was popular for different reasons in the past. Tintern was an important industrial centre. There was a Roman ford here and later a ferry. Iron was readily available from the neighbouring Forest of Dean, while fast flowing streams produced the power and water needed for foundries to thrive. In the late seventeenth century 1,500 people were employed in the wire works here. The finished products could be shipped downstream directly via the tidal waters of the Wye. Then, in 1905, came the railway. Trains brought tourists from the nearby industrial valleys of south-eastern Wales and from further afield.

I From the car park follow the path by the river upstream. This leads past some houses and soon on to the main road. Continue on the main road past the Abbey Mill. Then TURN RIGHT to cross the bridge over the river. The bridge was used to carry a branch from the Wye Valley Railway to serve Tintern wireworks. The line closed in 1935, many years after the wireworks itself. On the far side continue along the track and enjoy the views back across the river. At a signpost for 'Devil's Pulpit', TURN LEFT to follow a stony path slanting up the side of the hill past some metal bollards. There is a steep climb between holly bushes but soon you gain the narrow ridge, which has forced the Wye into a tight twist around the hill.

2 At a path junction by a stone wall, KEEP RIGHT and a few yards further KEEP RIGHT at a second fork. Soon leave what seems to be the main path and TURN LEFT. (The route straight ahead in fact soon begins to deteriorate and then to descend.) The stony path climbs steadily and can be muddy and slippery. When the gradient eases the path joins a wide forestry track. TURN RIGHT along this for a few yards and then immediately LEFT at a stone sign for the Devil's Pulpit. After a more level section, the route climbs steeply once more. The ascent finishes with a double bend that leads on to a T-junction at the top.

3 This is Offa's Dyke footpath. *The 177-mile long path runs from Chepstow to Prestatyn. For most of its route it follows the line of King Offa's ninth century earthwork built to mark out his Mercian kingdom from Wales. The path does not always follow the course of the Dyke itself. In some places the line of the earthwork is uncertain. But here the path and historic border coincide exactly. An impressive section of high dyke lies ahead, covered by trees.* TURN RIGHT and follow the dyke and the path along the ridge, with the wooded slope dropping steeply to the right. Just after a few steps, TURN RIGHT by a fingerpost and walk along the top of the dyke. Soon you come to the magnificent viewpoint at Devil's Pulpit. *The 'pulpit' itself is the stone pillar just below.* Having admired the view, continue along the Offa's Dyke path for about a mile. Just after a short but steepish descent, the path comes to a T-junction with a wide forest track.

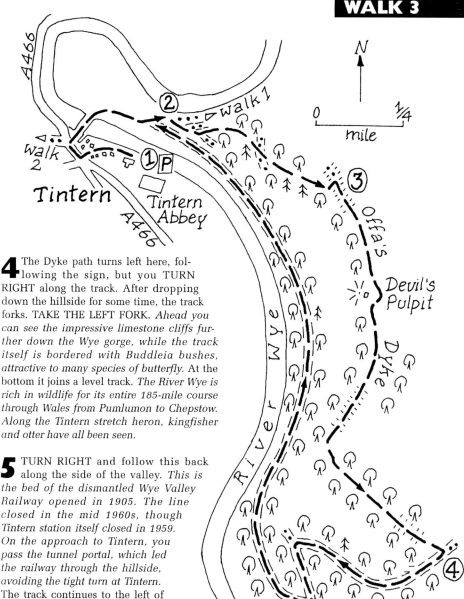

4 The Dyke path turns left here, following the sign, but you TURN RIGHT along the track. After dropping down the hillside for some time, the track forks. TAKE THE LEFT FORK. *Ahead you can see the impressive limestone cliffs further down the Wye gorge, while the track itself is bordered with Buddleia bushes, attractive to many species of butterfly. At the bottom it joins a level track. The River Wye is rich in wildlife for its entire 185-mile course through Wales from Pumlumon to Chepstow. Along the Tintern stretch heron, kingfisher and otter have all been seen.*

5 TURN RIGHT and follow this back along the side of the valley. *This is the bed of the dismantled Wye Valley Railway opened in 1905. The line closed in the mid 1960s, though Tintern station itself closed in 1959. On the approach to Tintern, you pass the tunnel portal, which led the railway through the hillside, avoiding the tight turn at Tintern. The track continues to the left of the tunnel and shortly rejoins the outward route. Return by the wire bridge to starting point.*

HIGH & LOW ALONG THE WYE

DESCRIPTION A 10 mile tour of the high ground and waterside meadows around the Wye valley. The outward route follows the Wye Valley Way high above the river, with stunning panoramas. A pastoral return route hugs the waterside, passing the villages of Bigsweir and Brockweir.
START Whitestone Car Park and Picnic Place. SO 524029. There are toilets here.
DIRECTIONS Whitestone is on the minor road between Tintern and Trellech.
PUBLIC TRANSPORT Bus 69 travels between Chepstow and Monmouth daily, including Sundays. It follows the line of the main road and there are stops at both Bigsweir (point 4) or across the river from Brockweir (just past point 5). You could begin and end the walk at either of these points if using the bus.

If you want a shorter circuit from Whitestone car park, follow the red markers for the ¾ mile 'Wonders of Whitestone' walk. This is way marked by the Forestry Commission.

I Follow the Wye Valley Walk direction signs north from the end of the car park. The ground slopes steeply away to the Wye on your right. You soon pass a viewpoint on the right and another after about ¼ mile. At the second point, a board records the visit of William Wordsworth. *Although usually associated with his native Lake District, Wordsworth wrote a poem here with the descriptive but unimaginative title 'Lines written a few miles above Tintern Abbey' in 1798. Whether the literary association inspires you or not, the view certainly will,* looking upriver to Bigsweir and across to Gloucestershire on the other bank. The path turns to the LEFT at the viewpoint and soon comes to a junction.

2 The short 'red' route heads back left here but for the main walk TURN RIGHT, following a yellow arrow for the Wye Valley Walk which now continues gently up hill.

After a while the path becomes a walled lane. At a junction of lanes, keep STRAIGHT AHEAD ignoring side turnings. Cross a stream and notice the waterfall (Cleddon Falls) on your right. Cross a lane by a house and continue on the Wye Valley Walk climbing steadily but easily through beech woods. At a diagonal junction keep STRAIGHT AHEAD on the bridleway, now more firm and level, along a wide avenue. *A variety of trees, oak, birch, beech and Scots pine, echo with bird song.* Notice a further viewpoint, named 'Duchess Ride' *after a local aristocrat who enjoyed travelling through the woods on horseback. The winding course of the Wye, fighting its way through the wooded gorge, can be traced down to its merger with the Severn near Chepstow. You may catch a glimpse of the Severn Bridge.* After an open area planted with saplings, pass through a gate and continue on the bridleway between two fences. A further gate leads on to a surfaced lane. Follow this between hedges. Carry straight ahead when it joins a wider lane at a bend. The lane begins to descend slightly. Immediately beyond the stone posted gateway to Duke's House, BEAR RIGHT and walk down a footpath through the trees. WATCH OUT here. There is a yellow marker on a nearby pole, but it could easily be missed. This path becomes a sunken lane and is still the Wye Valley Walk. Continue to follow it, bearing left at a junction by a house, on to a good track. The track reaches a road by a large grass area. TURN RIGHT and follow the road downhill. At the bottom, the road finishes at a gate to a property called 'The Folly'. A sign indicates that the path TURNS RIGHT here and the route twists down steeply on a rutted path through the woods. It widens out at a junction.

3 Ignore the wide track to the left. Instead CONTINUE STRAIGHT AHEAD, on down another steep rutted path, signposted as the Wye Valley Walk to the Whitebrook Road. But it is just a short distance to a lane. TURN RIGHT and follow this quiet road down towards the river. It swings right and continues along the floor of the valley, never far from the Wye. Continue for about a mile until it joins the main road near Bigsweir

Bridge. There is a bus stop here, offering an alternative start and finish to the walk.

4 Cross the main road and TURN LEFT following the footpath over Bigsweir Bridge and into England. At the far side, immediately TURN RIGHT on to Offa's Dyke Footpath. Follow the riverside path, sometimes a track, all the way to Brockweir, about 3 miles distant. *After a wooded section, there are open meadows with good views across to Llandogo.*

5 *Brockweir has a pub. There is also a community shop and café a few yards up the lane to your left.* To continue on the walk, TURN RIGHT to cross Brockweir Bridge back into Wales. At the far side TURN RIGHT along the main road for just a few yards. There is another bus stop here. Opposite the shelter, BEAR LEFT up a woodland footpath marked with a board, 'Wye Valley Walk'. Follow the path as it climbs through the trees, soon turning back left and then right again up some steps. The gradient eases and it continues next to a clawdd and then on through the middle of woodland. After some time, the path descends to a road by a house. TURN RIGHT for about 200 yards. By the entrance to a scout activity centre, TURN RIGHT to follow the Wye Valley Walk on a path through the woods. *This is a marshy area of woodland amid birch and holly trees.* When you come to another road, TURN SHARP LEFT along it for about 100 yards. Then TURN RIGHT back into the woods again to reach the Whitestones Car Park.

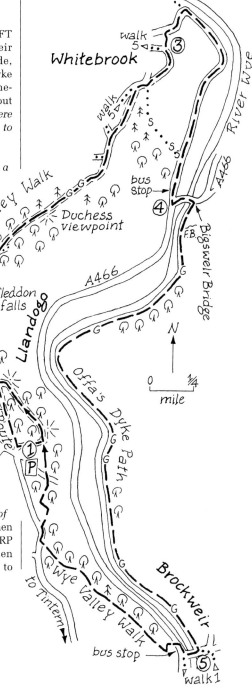

THE VALLEY OF THE WHITE BROOK

DESCRIPTION A 5 mile circuit around Whitebrook, whose forceful torrents once powered a series of paper mills and drove a great industrial valley. Today the picturesque remains have been reclaimed by ivy and moss, or restored as attractive homes. But history still adds texture to the great natural beauty of this minor tributary of the mighty Wye.

START Manor Wood Forestry Commission Car Park, The Narth. SO 528059.

DIRECTIONS Trellech lies on the B4293 between Monmouth and Chepstow. From the village take the road towards The Narth. After 1½ miles, bear right up a lane signposted to Pen-y-fan only. There is a Forestry Commission sign for Manor Wood on the left after ½ mile. Follow the track down to the small parking area.

PUBLIC TRANSPORT Bus 65 Monmouth – Chepstow via Trellech and The Narth. Around every 2 hours Mondays to Saturdays. It stops at Maryland (point **4** on the walk). You could start here instead. No Sunday service.

I Follow the track from the parking area back up to the road. Just before the lane, TURN LEFT to follow a byway between holly bushes. After passing a house, it returns to the lane in front of a chalet park. TURN LEFT and continue down the narrow road, enjoying views across the Wye Valley. Soon the road forks at the top of an open grassy area, Pen-y-fan Green. BEAR RIGHT down the right hand side of the green and twist down below some large houses. You are soon joined by the Wye Valley Walk (and **Walk 4**) from a path on the right. Notice the view down towards Bigsweir Bridge. At the bottom, the road ends at a private gate to 'The Folly'. A sign indicates that the path TURNS RIGHT here and the route then snakes down steeply on a rutted path through the woods. It widens out at a junction with a track.

2 TURN LEFT and follow the track past a house and onto a road junction. BEAR LEFT along the road, past a phone box and converted chapel. Immediately after the old chapel, take a track to the RIGHT crossing the brook and immediately come to a T-junction on the far side of the bridge. TURN LEFT following the sign to Pwllplythin Wood and Colonel's Park. Continue along a good track which follows the brook uphill past scattered houses and the remains of old mills. A wooded hillside rises steeply to the right as the track continues to ascend a charming wooded ravine. Immediately before the track crosses the brook, and just before it meets the road, BEAR RIGHT towards Colonel's Park. Stay on the right hand side of the stream, now on a narrower path. After a while the path diverts up hill around the grounds of a house. Follow the way as it zigzags steeply up through the woods. At the top, reach a more level area by the line of an old wall. TURN LEFT onto a path and follow its course through trees and holly bushes along the edge of the escarpment. After a while the trees thin out and you come to a stile. Cross this on to a track past some houses and on to a road. TURN LEFT and in a few yards reach a red phone box and a road junction.

Trellech Common

3 TURN LEFT and follow the road for just over 100 yards. Opposite a landscaped ruin, TURN RIGHT along a lane banned to motor vehicles. Continue past some bollards and at the top TURN LEFT along a road, ignoring the bridleway straight ahead. Continue along the road for only about 50 yards. Opposite the first house, BEAR RIGHT along a clear track through the woods. *This is Trellech Common.* After a while you join a wider forestry track which leads on to the road at Maryland. There is a bus stop here.

4 Cross the road and continue along a lane through the hamlet of Maryland. At the end of the tarmac a track continues into the forest signed towards Llandogo. At the first

10

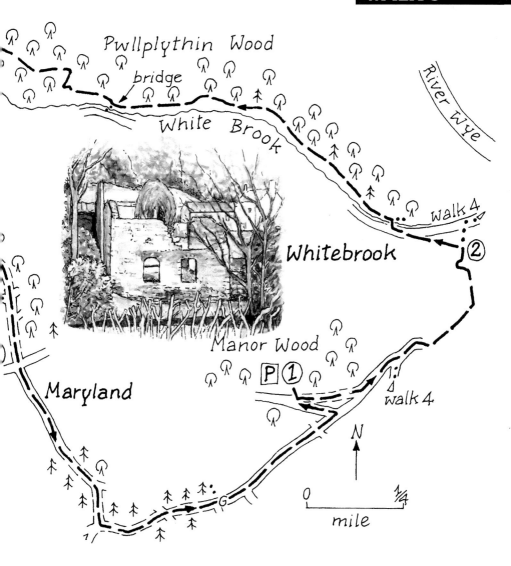

major junction, TURN LEFT along another track. *This is a very pleasant, easy going route through a variety of trees and with glimpses of open country beyond.* At the end of the forest, a gateway leads on to a quiet road, the terminus of the route to the picturesque hamlet of Pen-y-fan. Continue along the route, which drops down to a junction. TURN LEFT here and in about **300** yards reach the entrance to Manor Wood Car Park.

W*hitebrook*. *Like nearby Tintern, Whitebrook was once the hub of industrial activity. The fast flowing White Brook provided the power for mills, and you can see many of the remains today between points 2 and 3 on this walk. A wireworks operated here in the seventeenth century. During the middle of the eighteenth century, paper mills predominated and the industry continued until about 1880.*

THE RED BROOK
&
THE CATHEDRAL
OF THE FOREST

DESCRIPTION The elements that forged the Forest's history echo on this 5¼ mile circuit of Dean's western march. The iron-tinted water has given Redbrook its name; the stone has bequeathed the Forest a 'cathedral'; the trees have covered the sandstone escarpment that dives down to the Wye. This is border country. And just nearby, over a millennium ago, the Mercian King Offa used the border earth to mould a great boundary fortification.

START Redbrook village. There is a rough parking area on the west side of the main road. SO 536099, though there are also other possible places to leave a car in the village.

DIRECTIONS Redbrook is 3 miles south of Monmouth on the A466 towards Chepstow.

PUBLIC TRANSPORT Bus 69 Chepstow – Tintern – Redbrook - Monmouth for the start of the walk. Daily service including Sundays. Bus 65 Chepstow – Trellech – Monmouth for Pentwyn (point 4). No Sunday service.

I Follow a lane that leaves the main road between the school and the village hall. (The school is next to the church). The lane climbs steeply away from the village. The tarmac finishes at the last house and a track continues along a sunken way, bedecked by hart's tongue ferns. The route climbs steadily through woodland with glimpses of the valley below. It levels out as it joins another track. Continue to a fork. Here keep on the main track, BEARING LEFT and resuming the climb. At the top of the hill, emerge from the trees at a junction. Ignore the track crossing our route and carry on ahead VEERING LEFT to descend a green lane between tree-lined banks. The sunken track ends at some chicken coops on the edge of Newland village.

2 At this point the walk takes a RIGHT TURN by Valley Lodge bungalow with a sign indicating 'Restricted Byway'. However you may want to spend a little time exploring Newland village. To get there carry on past the bungalow and take the first left, Savage Hill. It is very steep, but short. At the top lies the village centre, an intriguing collection of houses arranged around the enormous parish church, known as the 'Cathedral of the Forest'. *It owes this venerable epithet to its size and historic significance. The church was established by a Norman, Robert de Wakering in the thirteenth century. In 1305, the scourge of the Welsh and Scots, English king Edward Longshanks founded a chantry in a small chapel by the south porch. Opposite the church is a row of almshouses dating back to the fifteenth century.* After your foray into Newland village, return to Valley Lodge at point **2**, by the same route. From here, follow the byway which is also an access road for some farms. It passes a sewage works but then continues on a gentle line just above the attractive Valley Brook. *This watercourse has carved a strange and sinuous course around the Old Red Sandstone ridge to your right. It first heads south but then, beyond point **3**, reverses its original intention, turning north to carve a trench through to Redbrook and the River Wye. Originally the Valley Brook was known as the Lower Red Brook (the Upper Brook being just to the north of the village – see **Walk 8**).*

3 After nearly a mile you approach Lodges Farm. Just before it, cross a bridge over the stream and then TURN RIGHT to pass below the farm buildings. Pass through a gate and continue along the byway as it curves around the valley which meanders a full 180 degrees to face north. After another house you soon pass an ornamental lake, attracting a variety of birds. There is no shortage of pheasants around here either!

4 Where the track forks BEAR LEFT keeping to the restricted bridleway (though the other route offers an alternative return to Redbrook). Cross a bridge and climb past some houses. After the gate there is a fork. BEAR RIGHT to stay on the 'restricted

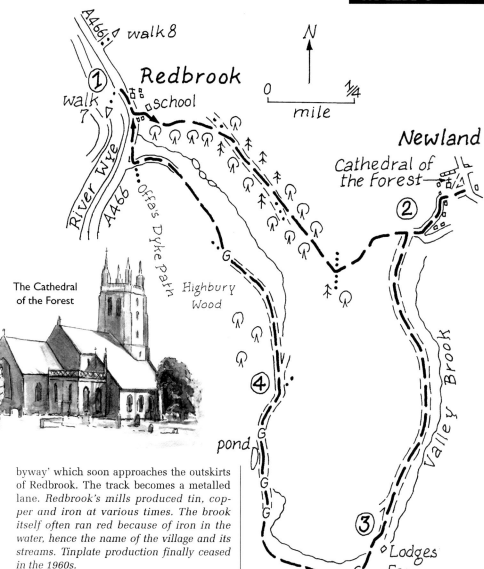

The Cathedral of the Forest

byway' which soon approaches the outskirts of Redbrook. The track becomes a metalled lane. *Redbrook's mills produced tin, copper and iron at various times. The brook itself often ran red because of iron in the water, hence the name of the village and its streams. Tinplate production finally ceased in the 1960s.*

As it curves to the left the lane crosses Offa's Dyke Path. *This long distance footpath runs for over 170 miles from Chepstow to Prestatyn. For much of its route it follows the course and remains of the ninth century border earthwork built by King Offa of Mercia. Just south of here, around Highbury Wood, is an impressive section of dyke, marked by yew trees. There are a num-* ber *of other vestiges of the dyke along this side of the Wye Valley between Chepstow and Monmouth. Beyond Monmouth little archaeological evidence remains until a further 40 miles north where the dyke and ditch become visible again around Knighton.* TURN RIGHT here to follow the long distance footpath a few yards down some steps into Redbrook village.

WALK 7

PENALLT, PENTWYN & HAEL WOOD

DESCRIPTION This 7½ mile walk starts in England but is almost entirely in Wales, using a foot crossing of the Wye to negotiate the international border in the first few yards. An initial riverside path leads to a steep climb up to the old village of Penallt with some great views. An undulating perambulation explores the attractive wooded hills that flank the Wye's western bank. The final section descends through forest to return along the riverbank using the track of the Wye Valley's former railway.

START Redbrook village. There is a rough parking area on the west side of the main road. SO 536099, though there are also other possible places to leave a car in the village.

DIRECTIONS Redbrook is 3 miles south of Monmouth on the A466 towards Chepstow.

PUBLIC TRANSPORT Bus 69 Chepstow – Tintern – Redbrook – Monmouth for the start of the walk. Daily service including Sundays. Bus 65 Chepstow – Trellech – Monmouth for Pentwyn (point 4). No Sunday service.

I From the car park in Redbrook, walk to the old bridge that spans the Wye. Cross the footbridge, strapped to the remnant of the railway bridge that carried the Wye Valley Railway over the water. *The station in Redbrook opened with the line in 1876, but Penallt had to wait until 1931 for a halt on the Welsh side of the river, just ¼ mile from Redbrook. This must have been one of the shortest distances between stations anywhere in Britain. The line closed to passengers in 1959.* On the far side of the river TURN RIGHT and follow the road past the Boat Inn. Just past the pub go through a gate on the RIGHT HAND side of the lane and follow the riverside footpath. This hugs the Wye with the wooded hills of Gwent rising up to your left and the Forest of Dean on the far side. The meadows give way to a small wood and the path now clings to the waterside below

the escarpment. Near the end of the wood, BEAR LEFT and climb steeply up a bridle-way marked with arrows. Cross a driveway and keep on the route of the footpath now veering to the right up a walled track. When this reaches a road, TURN RIGHT and continue to climb up the hillside to a sharp bend at the top. This is the old village of Penallt.

2 At this corner, leave the road, BEARING RIGHT to follow a footpath sign for Troy. The way leads through the churchyard of Penallt old church. At the far side a stile indicates the path which follows the top side of a field with stunning views north towards Monmouth. At the top of the field, TURN SHARP LEFT through a gate. Follow the broad grassy track below some houses and just above the church. It soon becomes a walled lane. Ignore a footpath bearing left down the hill and continue on the main track climbing up below a house. Follow the driveway out through the gate and at the end BEAR RIGHT to join the road.

3 The next section sounds complicated but it is more straightforward than it appears! There is a sequence of quiet lanes and footpaths. Follow these instructions carefully and you should have no problems. Follow the road. About 100 yards after it bends sharply to the right, TURN LEFT down a footpath just past a horse-jumping arena. The path leaves the driveway immediately and goes through a gate and down a small field. A further gate leads to a walled lane which soon reaches the bottom of the valley at a lovely secluded spot near a house. Continue straight ahead, crossing the driveway to another stile. A short ascent leads to a road. TURN LEFT and follow this to a road junction in front of a farm. TURN SHARP RIGHT and climb the lane past another farm and an orchard to another road junction. TURN RIGHT. After about 200 yards, TURN LEFT along a broad track signed for Pentwyn and Pen-y-garn. In another 300 yards, TURN LEFT crossing a stile onto a footpath along the side of a field. At the end of the field it becomes an enclosed footpath which then leads to a road junction in Pen-twyn. TURN RIGHT and follow the road through the village and past the war memorial.

4 At the next cross roads (Pentwyn Cross), carry on straight ahead for a few yards. Then BEAR LEFT, off the road, following a footpath towards Tre Gagle. Follow this through landscaped parkland. It soon joins a driveway. Where this veers left into the buildings, carry on STRAIGHT AHEAD passing in front of a series of grand houses and an old chapel. At the end of the manicured grounds, a kissing gate leads into a much wilder piece of land with lots of bracken. Take the LEFT FORK and follow the path below a bungalow and on to a road.

5 KEEP STRAIGHT AHEAD on to the road, which then descends the hill. Maintain this direction, keeping on the lane through a series of junctions, *passing a red pillar box and a house with an interesting weather vane that leaves no doubt about its nationality.* Pass a 'no through road' sign and continue to the end of the lane at a forest entrance. Ignore the bridleway sign to the right. Instead keep STRAIGHT ON along a woodland path which soon descends through the woods. Where it joins a broad forest track, TURN LEFT to join it.

6 At the nape of the ridge, you come to a junction of tracks. Whitebrook lies down in front, but instead TURN SHARP LEFT to follow the main track which now descends the steep slope of the Wye Valley diagonally. It reaches the bank of the river in about a mile. TURN LEFT here to join the Wye Valley Walk. *From this point you are also walking on the track of the Wye Valley railway.* Follow this back to the footbridge near the Boat Inn and cross the river back to Redbrook.

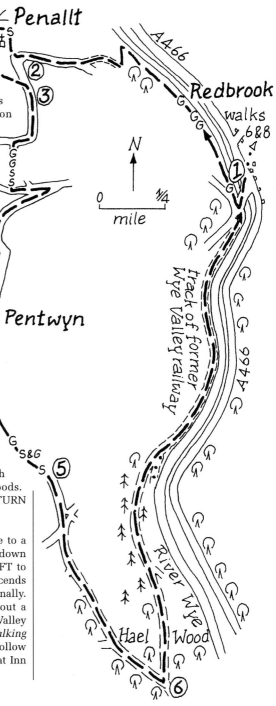

AROUND THE KYMIN

DESCRIPTION Water features strongly in this 6-mile excursion from Monmouth. The outward leg accompanies the fast flowing Wye on an attractive riverside path leading to the English border at Redbrook. A climb up the wooded slopes of the Kymin reveals an unlikely 'temple' commemorating conflicts in much more salty waters. Next door, a unique Georgian banqueting house crowns the summit with panoramic views across the Wye.

START Monmouth Bridge (the A4136 Wye bridge, not the more famous and photogenic Monnow Bridge). SO 512127.

DIRECTIONS Park at one of several pay and display car parks in the town and walk to the bridge. Cross the A40 by using the subway to reach Monmouth Bridge.

PUBLIC TRANSPORT Regular buses serve Monmouth from neighbouring areas, terminating at the bus station at the other end of the town near the Monnow Bridge.

I Cross the River Wye on the road towards the Forest of Dean from the traffic lights. On the far side of the river, TURN RIGHT following a signpost for the Wye Valley Walk. The path passes a sewage pumping station but then continues between the river and a recreation field. *High above to your left you should be able to see the Round Tower at the Kymin, the highest point of this walk. On a sunny day, its white paint glistens, crowning the wooded ridge above the town. The Monnow joins the Wye from the opposite side.* You soon pass under the remains of an iron viaduct and afterwards, the stub of a stone bridge. Both these abandoned crossings carried railways over the river to Monmouth Troy station and on to Pontypool. *The iron bridge was built for the Ross and Monmouth railway, which also served Monmouth May Hill station, close to where you started the walk. The track bed now provides a cycle way as far as Symond's Yat. The stone bridge brought trains north from Chepstow along*

the picturesque Wye Valley Railway. Both routes were constructed in the 1870s but closed between 1959 and 1964. After another sewage works, you leave the woods to arrive at an open field next to the river. The Wye is in a hurry, tumbling quickly along the final phase of its journey from Pumlimon to Chepstow. As it swings right on a more southerly course, you re-enter woodland. In spring, a carpet of wood anemones and bluebells decorates the earthen path as it weaves among the trees at the water's edge. After a river monitoring station, the way is more open. Just before Redbook, the path is squeezed from its waterside terrace and has to continue along the main road for about 200 yards. Take care here.

2 As you enter the village of Redbrook, just before you cross the border into England, TURN LEFT along a side road, signposted to Clearwell and Newland. This climbs away from the river. You pass under an arch. *Trains once steamed up the steep and twisty branch line to Coleford, built in 1884. This section had a short lived history and was closed during the first world war. After the arch, Offa's Dyke long distance footpath joins us from the right and stays with us throughout the remainder of the walk. The 177-mile long path runs from Chepstow to Prestatyn. For most of its route it follows the line of King Offa's ninth century earthwork built to mark out his Mercian kingdom from Wales. A little further up, a wooden signpost, marked with a national trail logo, indicates the way to Monmouth.* BEAR LEFT up this narrow lane as it slants up the side of the little valley. As the lane swings left further up, you re-cross the line of the Coleford railway. *If you look carefully over the fence you can see evidence of the line below you. The tarmac ends at Duffield's Farm but the track continues and views extend across the Wye Valley and the Forest of Dean. The border with England runs along the bottom of the valley to your right, below the trees of the forest.*

3 The track ends at a house on the left, Cockshoot Ash Barn and changes into a footpath. Immediately after the house, be careful not to miss a gate in the fence to

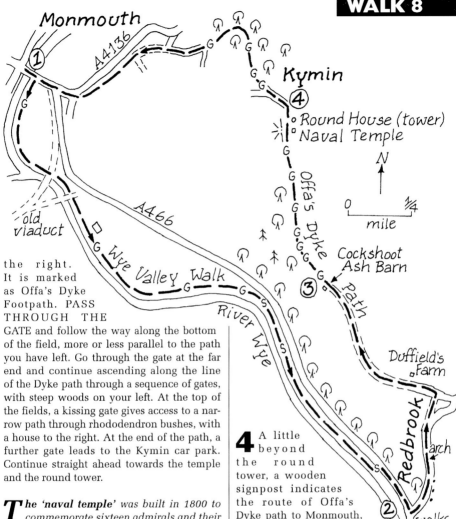

Monmouth

Kymin

④

° Round House (tower)
° Naval Temple

N

Offa's Dyke

0   ¼
        mile

old viaduct

Wye Valley Walk

Cockshoot
Ash Barn

③

River Wye

Duffield's
Farm

Redbrook

②

walks
6 & 7

arch

the right. It is marked as Offa's Dyke Footpath. PASS THROUGH THE GATE and follow the way along the bottom of the field, more or less parallel to the path you have left. Go through the gate at the far end and continue ascending along the line of the Dyke path through a sequence of gates, with steep woods on your left. At the top of the fields, a kissing gate gives access to a narrow path through rhododendron bushes, with a house to the right. At the end of the path, a further gate leads to the Kymin car park. Continue straight ahead towards the temple and the round tower.

*T*he 'naval temple' was built in 1800 to commemorate sixteen admirals and their exploits in the eighteenth century, chiefly at the expense of the French. The 'temple' is built high up on the ridge above the eastern bank of the Wye, known as the Kymin. Nelson visited Monmouth in 1802, after a more modest waterborne cruise down river from Ross. For many years before this, the 'gentlemen' of Monmouth had enjoyed open-air lunch parties on the Kymin. The Round Tower was built in 1794 as a banqueting house so they could avoid the 'inclement weather'. Today owned by the National Trust, the Kymin is still a great place for picnics, with pleasant woodland walks and outstanding views over Monmouth and the Black Mountains.

4 A little beyond the round tower, a wooden signpost indicates the route of Offa's Dyke path to Monmouth, LEFT from the top, down some stone steps through the woods. A gate leads on to a tarmac access road. Follow this down hill for a few yards before TURNING RIGHT through another gate and heading down a field. Continue to FOLLOW THE PATH down hill through the woodland. When you join a surfaced lane, follow this until it turns back sharply to the right. CONTINUE AHEAD HERE on to an access road, until this veers to the left. Instead, CONTINUE AHEAD down a footpath dropping through a final section of woodland. At the main road, TURN LEFT to return to Monmouth's Wye Bridge.

17

THE DOWARD

DESCRIPTION The Doward is an interesting outcrop of quartz and limestone towering above the Wye. It is sandwiched between the busy A40 and the tourist honey pot of Symond's Yat, yet it retains a craggy isolation and quiet independence. Sidelined from the tourist trunk routes, limestone quarries and neighbouring grasslands provide great habitats for butterflies. The area is characterised by many old stone walls, now dilapidated and topped with beech hedges. There is a complex web of byways and footpaths almost impossible to decipher on maps or to find on the ground. However, this 4-mile walk provides an exhilarating exploration of a fascinating terrain above the Wye Gorge before descending to a waterside promenade through Symond's Yat West.

START Small parking area at entrance to White Rocks Nature Reserve. SO 548157

DIRECTIONS The easiest approach is from the A40 at Whitchurch, mid way between Ross and Monmouth. Initially, follow the sign to Symond's Yat West. But then follow a signpost to Crocker's Ash and Doward. In one mile turn left at a sign to Doward. Follow this narrow lane until a very sharp left hand bend by the entrance to Doward Park camp site. Just round the bend, on the right, there is a small parking area at the entrance to White Rocks Nature Reserve. You could start the walk from Symond's Yat West (point **5**) but parking is very limited.

PUBLIC TRANSPORT There are no buses to the Doward, though you could start the walk from Symond's Yat West and use Bus 34 Ross-Monmouth.

*W*hite Rocks Nature Reserve *is managed by Herefordshire Nature Trust. It is a former limestone quarry with surrounding woodland. Wild flowers, orchids and butterflies thrive here.*

I From the small car park, follow the lane back down hill past the campsite entrance and round the sharp bend to the right. About 200 yards after the bend, TURN SHARP LEFT down a footpath, almost doubling back. Pass a nature reserve sign and continue along the path as it descends through beech woodland and soon arrives in an old quarry. Follow the yellow arrow veering RIGHT to leave the quarry. *You soon pass King Arthur's Cave and series of small caves in the limestone cliffs on the left of the path.*

2 At the end of the cliffs, carry on down through the woodlands, now following the yellow way markers of the Highmeadow Trail. The route continues to descend for a while, but then BEARS LEFT at an arrow up a small rocky scar. Now on the right ground falls precipitously away to the Wye Gorge and care is needed in places. The path is narrow, but clear and easy. Keep following the arrows. In a small dip these lead the trail LEFT uphill and then RIGHT on a narrower path in advance of a large disused quarry. Later the path crosses a couple of gravel tracks, but always maintains the same direction, following the way markers until it ends at a T-junction with a major track. TURN LEFT here, still following the Highmeadow trail. The track drops past a small rocky scar and then hugs the side of the gorge. An old shaft is passed on the left. Keep STRAIGHT AHEAD, now descending more steadily on a good track with the sound of the rapids in the river below.

3 The track comes to another T-junction. Both ways offer descents. The Highmeadow Trail turns right to head towards Biblins. However, you TURN LEFT following the wider track downhill. *The houses of Symond's Yat can be glimpsed below through the trees.* At a large disused quarry, keep on the main track as it contours above some houses and reaches a lane.

4 TURN SHARP RIGHT and walk carefully down the narrow road. The sheer cliffs on the east bank of the river are now dramatically evident. Follow the road as it TWISTS BACK TO THE LEFT and becomes even narrower at a sign to Symond's Yat West. The yellow lines seem superfluous as there is little room between them for a bicycle, never mind a parked car. The route now becomes

18

a byway and follows the river a little above the water's edge. Notice the turning to the ferry across to the pub on the east bank. *A little further on another ferry crosses the river, this time to the Olde Ferrie Inne on this side.* Continue up Washings Lane to the road.

5 Follow the road for a short distance. Just past the entrance to Paddocks Hotel and near a phone box, BEAR LEFT up Ashes Lane. When you reach Stonewall Cottage, TURN SHARP LEFT at a junction, and continue to climb the hill diagonally, now in the opposite direction. The lane becomes a track. Where it splits, take the UPPER FORK. Soon the houses finish and the path goes through

Symond's Yat West

woodland. You reach a junction and find the lane has been given the name of 'Drag Road', perhaps appropriate! Keep STRAIGHT ON here now along a footpath, still climbing diagonally. It goes around a house then on up a driveway to reach Mine Pitts Lane.

6 At the junction, KEEP STRAIGHT ON past a huge beech tree on an island in the middle of the junction. Continue along the quiet tarmac lane, now level. It twists left

and then back to the right. On this right hand bend, leave the lane and continue AHEAD following a byway sign in to May Bush Lane. After about 250 yards, watch out for a footpath to the RIGHT. There is no signpost at its junction, but a few yards along it there is a sign for the White Rocks Nature Reserve. Carry on LEFT past the sign, then immediately take the RIGHT HAND path through a more open area. This leads to the far side of the reserve and the small car park.

GOODRICH & COPPETT HILL

DESCRIPTION There are two distinct sections to this 6½-mile walk. The outward leg follows a level course along the banks of the River Wye. The return route climbs onto the heathland ridge of Coppett Hill, now managed as a nature reserve. You may like to take the opportunity to visit nearby Goodrich Castle.

START Post Office in Goodrich Village. SO 575194. There is a car park and picnic area at nearby Goodrich Castle. There is a parking fee payable here and it closes at 5 pm. Otherwise, there is some space to park sensibly in the village.

DIRECTIONS Goodrich village is reached easily from the A40 between Monmouth and Ross or the B5234 between Ross and Lydbrook.

PUBLIC TRANSPORT Bus 34 serves Goodrich from Ross and Monmouth. There is no Sunday or Bank Holiday service.

I Start from the Post Office and bus stop in the village. Take the 'no through road' signposted to Courtfield and Welsh Bicknor. At the end of the houses, cross a bridge over another road below. At the far side of the bridge, look carefully for a path down steps to the LEFT. This descends to the lower road. Follow this road down the hill towards the river, passing Flanesford Priory on the left. *A priory was established here in the fourteenth century. Following Henry VIII's dissolution of the monasteries, the site later became a farm before being refurbished as holiday apartments in 1980.* There is a good pavement and you soon reach Kerne Bridge.

2 Immediately before the bridge, TURN RIGHT at a fingerpost for the Wye Valley Walk. A few steps lead down to a riverside path alongside a field. For a short way, there may be some long grass but as you reach the woods, the path improves. Climb a short flight of steps to reach a terrace a little above the river. *Near a half-timbered house a bridge used to bring the Ross and Monmouth*

Railway across the Wye. Nature has reclaimed the track bed since closure in 1965, but if you look carefully you will see evidence of the former line in the form of old concrete fence posts. After about 1/4 mile the railway turned through Lydbrook Tunnel under the steep hillside on its way to Monmouth, short-cutting the great loop of the river followed by this walk. The good path continues through Thomas Wood, attractive mature woodland. At the end of the woods, a gateway leads to a riverside meadow. GO THROUGH THIS, ignoring the track that climbs to the right through the woods. The path now passes through open grassland next to the water, with a great wall of trees guarding the slope to the right. As you begin to curve round to the right, the houses of Lydbrook climb the opposite bank. *The river is now the county boundary between Herefordshire o n this side, and Gloucestershire on the other.*

3 As you come towards the furthest point on the loop, a line of trees stretches up the slope along a mound of earth between two fields. Leave the riverside path here and follow the yellow footpath arrow to the RIGHT alongside this row of trees. At the top of the field, go through a gate on to a track between trees and a wall. *You soon pass the disused buildings of Courtfield on your left. The site has a long historical pedigree, a young but previous Prince Harry (later Henry V) staying here. The present manor house dates from the nineteenth century and Courtfield was a retreat and training centre for priests until closure in 2005.* The track continues along the crest of the hill *with good views down to the river and across to Lydbrook on the Gloucestershire bank.* The lane joins a quiet tarmac road, which comes up from Welsh Bicknor youth hostel. *Deep underground is Lydbrook Tunnel which carried the Ross and Monmouth Railway under the* *hill. Although now in Herefordshire, Welsh Bicknor was a detached parish of Monmouthshire until the maps were tidied up in the mid nineteenth century.* Pass through some open grazing land and then cross a cattle grid, re-entering woodland. Soon there are the remains of a small quarry on the left. Next to this is a sign for Coppett Hill Nature Reserve.

5 TURN SHARP RIGHT to follow another wide grass track back towards Goodrich. It soon descends down the side of Coppett Hill. Pass some houses and then reach a small road. Follow this to a triangular junction. TURN LEFT to follow the road back to the starting point, with views right to Kerne Bridge and left to the graceful spire of Goodrich church.

G oodrich Castle was founded by Godric, a Saxon thegn (land owner), in the eleventh century. Its long history includes being on both sides in the English Civil War. The mortar, Roaring Meg, dates from this time and is now installed in the castle grounds. There is a café and shop here and the site is now in the care of English Heritage (entry charge).

4 BEAR LEFT to climb the clear sunken footpath that climbs up the hill. It ascends through woods, later winding beside an old wall, until it reaches the top. This is Coppett Hill, which stretches for 1½ miles south from here. A trig point caps the nape of the ridge. TURN LEFT at the OS column, climbing a few yards to the 'Folly', the remains of a small stone building. *From here there are commanding views over Goodrich and Symond's Yat. The Wye winds its tortuous course between the wooded hills, as if wriggling to put off its inevitable union with its senior cousin, the Severn, a few miles downstream.* Continue along the good grassy track beyond the folly along the crest of the ridge with woodland to the left and an expansive panorama to the right. The woods on the left finish near a slight depression in the path. There is a junction of paths here, by some electricity wires.

C oppett Hill is a steep sided sandstone ridge, with quartz and limestone strata. It is managed as a local nature reserve. At least 30 species of butterfly have been observed here, including the pearl-bordered fritillary. It is also a good habitat for birds of prey such as peregrine and sparrow hawk. For more information, see www.coppett-hill. org.uk and www.wyevalleyaonb.org.uk.

21

THE PLACE OF THE STONES

DESCRIPTION Staunton crowns the last outpost of England, a ridge overlooking the Wye and the hills of Gwent beyond. The village is built in a clearing of common heath land or 'meend' and surrounded by forest. The 'settlement of the stones', owes its name to the assortment of bronze and iron age standing stones in the vicinity. These walks visit two of them, the Long Stone and the Buckstone. Others include the Broadstones, to the west of the village, and the Suck Stone in the woods to the north.
Walk 11 (3¾ miles) traverses the southern part of Highmeadow Woods between Staunton and Christchurch.
Walk 12 (2¼ miles) explores the heath land around Staunton, and includes a panoramic view of the Wye Valley from its highest point at the Buckstone.
START Staunton church. SO 551126. There is no car park but space can be found off the main road in the village.
DIRECTIONS Staunton is on the A4136 three miles from Monmouth.
PUBLIC TRANSPORT Bus 35/35A Monmouth –Staunton – Coleford. Regular service Mon-Sat but no buses on Sundays.

WALK 11
LONG STONE & BRACELANDS

All Saints Church, Staunton crowns a strategic point on the crest of the ridge. The original building dates back to the twelfth century and one of its two fonts may have been re-sculpted from a Roman altar. David Mushet, an early industrial entrepreneur is buried in the churchyard (see Walk 14).

I Start at the church and cross the main road to a path marked by a sign 'Restricted Bridleway'. The enclosed lane leads across a field and then heads into the woods. The track levels out and drops slight-ly to a junction. TURN LEFT along this forest road, now following the yellow arrows of the Highmeadow Trail. You continue on this trail until point **3**, so the way-markers offer useful guidance. As the track nears the main road, it comes to another junction and swings around to the left. But, instead of following this, KEEP STRAIGHT AHEAD following a narrow but clear path through the trees. This angles through to the main A4136 road. Cross this busy road with care, TURN RIGHT and follow the verge for a few yards to reach the Long Stone, right on the edge of the road. *There is a local tale that this 7 feet high Bronze Age stone will bleed if pricked on the stroke of midnight.*

2 From the Stone, BEAR LEFT following the Highmeadow Trail along a narrow footpath. In 200 yards TURN LEFT to follow another path with drainage ditches either side. Soon come to a track and TURN RIGHT. Now follow this straight ahead. At a dip, cross another track and keep straight ahead on a footpath. The path curves round to the left, tracing the perimeter of the woods. When you come to a forest road TURN RIGHT through a barrier and then immediately LEFT keeping to the Highmeadow Trail, ignoring any side turnings. This routes you round the edge of the large Forestry Commission camp site at Christchurch.

3 At the end of the site, the path meets a metalled road. (This is also point 3 on Walk 13). Leave the Highmeadow Trail here and TURN SHARP LEFT down the road. Continue past a house and the entrance to Bracelands Camp site, keeping straight on when the road becomes a track. About 200 yards beyond this entrance, opposite a foot gate into the camping field, TURN LEFT

22

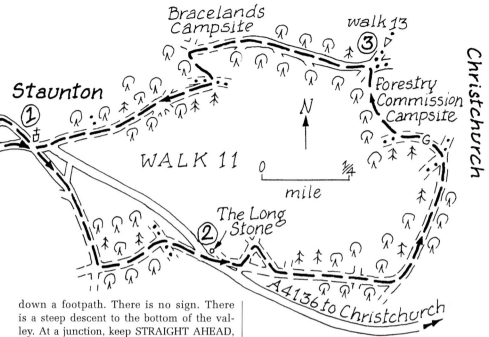

walk 13

down a footpath. There is no sign. There is a steep descent to the bottom of the valley. At a junction, keep STRAIGHT AHEAD, crossing a small stream and then curving round to the right following the line of some electricity wires. This soon becomes a broad track ascending the side of the hill. Near the top keep the line of the route, next to fields, and avoid right turnings. Soon the houses of Staunton appear and you arrive back at Staunton Church.

WALK 12
THE BUCKSTONE

I From the Church follow the main road through the village towards Monmouth. Just past the White Horse pub, BEAR LEFT up a no through road. After a few yards, come to a gate across the road. Cross the stile next to this and BEAR RIGHT steeply up a footpath beside a wall. This climbs steadily through oak woods. At the top there is a clearing next to a covered reservoir. *Over the wall are a couple of concrete pillars; one of these is a trig point marking the summit of the ridge. Just beyond is a large boulder*

known as the Buckstone. This vantage point offers grand views across the Wye into Wales. The border is just 300 yards below you.

2 From the top follow a track which curves down hill below the reservoir. Where this joins a road, TURN RIGHT and follow it to the end by a house. TURN LEFT in front of the gate to an adventure centre and follow the path down hill across the edge of heath land. At the bottom pass a house and come to a track.

3 TURN LEFT along a pleasant and easy lane towards Staunton. As you enter the village, just past the first house, TURN RIGHT down a narrow road. Follow this through the village back up to the church.

SYMOND'S YAT, MAILSCOT WOOD & THE RIVER WYE

DESCRIPTION A shady 6-mile tour through the eastern side of Highmeadow Woods, using good tracks and paths. The return follows the left bank of the Wye before climbing steeply back up to Yat Rock.

START Symond's Yat Forestry car park, SO 563156 Parking charge payable.

DIRECTIONS Symond's Yat is in two parts on opposite banks of the River Wye, appropriately named West and East. This walk begins high above Symond's Yat East, at Yat Rock. The easiest access is from the A4136 just north of Coleford. Follow the road from Berry Hill Pike through Christchurch. The route from the A40 at Whitchurch is narrow and steep. There are often delays and it is not recommended for anything other than small cars. There is an alternative start at Christchurch campsite (point 3). SO 567130. This avoids the narrow approaches to Symond's Yat and is also accessible by bus.

PUBLIC TRANSPORT Bus 30 Coleford – Gloucester serves Christchurch crossroads, close to point 3. Daily, including limited evening and Sunday service (Bus 31).

*Y*at Rock *pulls in the visitors today. But this is nothing new. It has been a tourist attraction for the last 200 years. Originally travellers arrived by boat, and later by train. The railway passes directly under the Yat Rock 'peninsula' through a tunnel far below. Now most visitors come by car and access is by narrow and busy lanes. If you visit on a bank holiday or summer Saturday you will see its popularity is certainly undiminished. But there's plenty of space in the woods around and you can quickly leave the crowds behind.*

I An ignominious start by the toilet block. From here follow the sign to the refreshment cabin and viewpoint, climbing gently up the stony track. You pass through an area of mounds and ditches. *This is the site of an Iron Age fort commanding views across the narrow Wye valley. Iron Age forts were generally used between the 6th century BC and the Roman conquest. This site may have been occupied even earlier.* Soon you come to another fingerpost in the disabled parking area. TURN RIGHT here, past the barrier and out through the disabled parking access road. Before this joins the main road, keep on the right hand side, following public footpath signs to the RIGHT of a collection of wooden buildings and a white house. Keep straight along on a good forest path, crossing two car park access roads. The woodland is quite open with some marshy areas at the side of the path, though the route is firm and clear.

2 The path splits at a big oak tree next to a wooden bench. Take the LEFT HAND FORK following the yellow arrow. Continue along this path as it passes a house (Mailscot Lodge) and on through the woods, more or less level. Ignore all side turnings to the right or left. *There are some good views as you contour along the edge of the slope through beech woodland.*

3 The path ends at a wooden barrier just before a small road, with a campsite on the other side. (This is also point 3 on **Walk 11**). Just before the barrier, TURN SHARP RIGHT down hill past a rope activity centre. Follow the path as it descends through mixed woodland with many mature beech trees. After a short while a broader track joins from the right. Carry on STRAIGHT AHEAD joining it. However, the main track soon veers left by some electricity wires. At this point carry STRAIGHT ON along a wide but earthier track. It soon drops again, this time through denser woodland, until it reaches a T-junction in a valley. TURN LEFT to follow a good track down the valley. *Hart's Tongue ferns, ramsons and other wild flowers carpet the coppiced beech woodland. At the bottom you reach the banks of the River Wye.*

4 TURN RIGHT following a sign to Symond's Yat East. There are two wide tracks running parallel at this point. This is the line of the Wye Valley railway and today serves as a section of the Wye Valley Walk. It is now also a cycle path running upstream from Monmouth to Symond's Yat. The lower of the two tracks is nearer the river. Soon you can branch left off the track to follow a path through a grassy sward next to the Wye. You emerge from this riverside terrace at a barrier leading into a car park.

5 On your right is the Royal Lodge Hotel, *offering food and drinks.* In front of the hotel, BEAR RIGHT along a narrow footpath signposted, 'Yat Rock ½'. This slants up quite steeply through woodland. Follow the yellow marker part way up to negotiate a zigzag. Steps aid progress as the climb continues up the side of the Wye gorge, with glimpses of the river below through the trees. A little further up, a fingerpost points the way SHARP RIGHT. Cross a track and continue following the line of the steps until you emerge right onto Yat Rock and the picnic site. *A refreshment cabin is here; you may feel you deserve to make use of it after your steep climb. There are great views across the Wye and the woodlands around.* To visit the crown of the Rock, cross a bridge over the road and follow the path LEFT to a viewpoint. *There is a toposcope here and the chance of seeing peregrine falcons that nest nearby. The RSPB has a display at peak times, and offers the loan of binoculars.* From the refreshment cabin, it is a short walk back to the car park and the starting point.

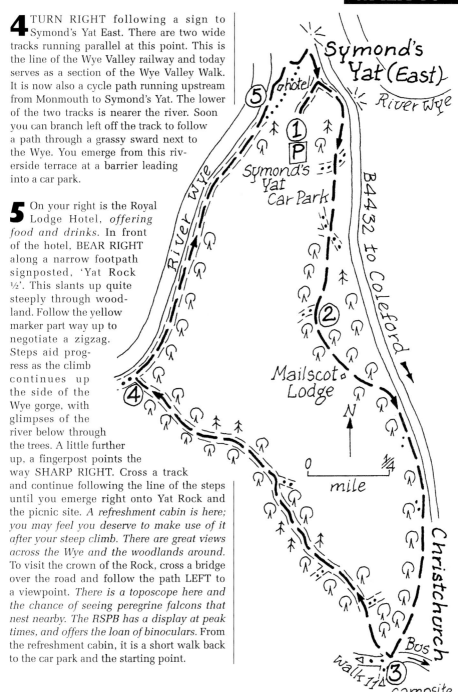

25

STONE, IRON & COAL IN THE HEART OF THE FOREST

DESCRIPTION Industrial enterprise and natural beauty are interwoven on this 5½ mile walk around the slopes of the Cannop valley. A groundbreaking ironworks, a complex network of tramways, disused quarries and memories of a tragic mining accident all resonate through the spectacular natural beauty of the forest.

START Car park at Fetter Hill, about 2 miles south of Coleford. SO 587086

DIRECTIONS From the traffic lights in the centre of Coleford take the B4228 southwards towards Chepstow. After about 200 yards, bear left to follow the road to Coalway. In Coalway keep straight on at the crossroads towards Parkend. Descend through the forest to a T-junction. Turn right and you will find the car park on the right after about 300 yards.

PUBLIC TRANSPORT The nearest convenient public transport is at Parkend, ½ mile from point **2**. Route 727 from Lydney operates Mon-Sat only.

I From the far side of the car park follow a wide stony track a short way past a barrier until another track crosses the path. TURN RIGHT to follow this gently down hill. *This is the line of the Coleford railway. It now forms a branch of the Forest cycleway network between Coleford and Parkend. Soon you pass Dark Hill Iron Works on your left. This is an important site in the history of the industrial revolution. David Mushet, a key local figure, produced iron here from the early nineteenth century. Much of the site has been conserved and interpretative displays outline its significance. The old railway used to cross the next road by a bridge. But this has long since disappeared and the cycleway loops round to negotiate it by a crossing.* CROSS THE ROAD WITH CARE AND CONTINUE on the opposite side. The

route of the dismantled railway continues downhill on a very steep gradient for a friction railway. *The line linked Monmouth, Coleford and Lydney.* In a while you pass the remains of Point Quarry on the left. *This impressive rock face was served by a tramway. The course of this is evident in places, and it passes underneath the railway line through a tunnel. You can see the portal as it emerges on the lower side of your route.*

2 A driveway crosses the cycle way just before a white house surrounded by a fence. TURN LEFT and then immediately leave the driveway to follow the public footpath marker indicating the Gloucestershire Way. *You are now entering Nagshead Nature Reserve. The RSPB reserve is home to a wide range of birds, including woodpeckers, redstarts and pied flycatchers. Buzzards and sparrow hawks may be seen overhead.* Cross a stile and then a forest drive, BEARING LEFT to follow the Gloucestershire Way footpath and also a nature trail sign. Keep straight on along this path through mature mixed woodland. Ignore a later nature trail sign to the left. A gate and a stile lead on to a forest road. Go STRAIGHT ON across an embankment for 50 yards. At this point the Gloucestershire Way turns right. But we leave that route here and instead TURN LEFT along a smaller footpath lined with stone sets.

3 Follow this footpath through a valley known as Bix Slade. *The stones once supported sleepers, as this is the course of a tramway that carried iron ore in the 1920s.* Cross an access track leading to a working quarry up to your right. *A few yards along the track to the left is a memorial to the four men who were killed by a flood, and to others who were trapped, in the Union Colliery in 1902. The pit entrance was situated near this point. It closed in the same year as the accident.* Keep STRAIGHT AHEAD, following the footpath as it bears right up through the woods. A line of electricity poles also guides the way and we still have the stone sets for company. *Further up, on the left, is an old airshaft, further evidence of the industrial history of the Forest.* The path

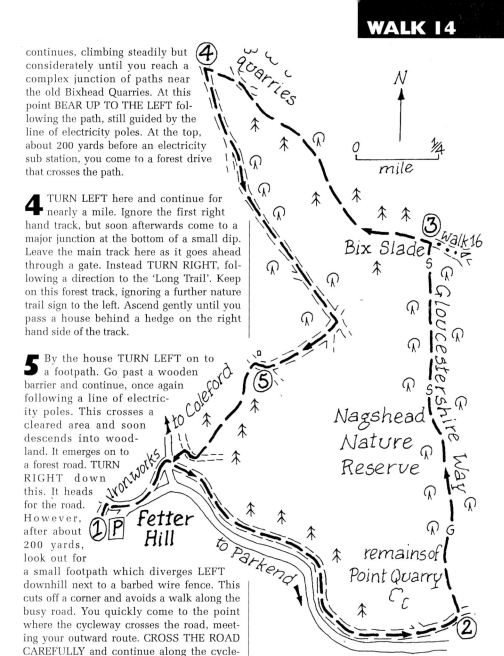

continues, climbing steadily but considerately until you reach a complex junction of paths near the old Bixhead Quarries. At this point BEAR UP TO THE LEFT following the path, still guided by the line of electricity poles. At the top, about 200 yards before an electricity sub station, you come to a forest drive that crosses the path.

4 TURN LEFT here and continue for nearly a mile. Ignore the first right hand track, but soon afterwards come to a major junction at the bottom of a small dip. Leave the main track here as it goes ahead through a gate. Instead TURN RIGHT, following a direction to the 'Long Trail'. Keep on this forest track, ignoring a further nature trail sign to the left. Ascend gently until you pass a house behind a hedge on the right hand side of the track.

5 By the house TURN LEFT on to a footpath. Go past a wooden barrier and continue, once again following a line of electricity poles. This crosses a cleared area and soon descends into woodland. It emerges on to a forest road. TURN RIGHT down this. It heads for the road. However, after about 200 yards, look out for a small footpath which diverges LEFT downhill next to a barbed wire fence. This cuts off a corner and avoids a walk along the busy road. You quickly come to the point where the cycleway crosses the road, meeting your outward route. CROSS THE ROAD CAREFULLY and continue along the cycleway past Dark Hill ironworks and back to the start point.

THE
MINERAL LOOP

DESCRIPTION The Forest of Dean was criss-crossed by railways and tramways that served the extensive mineral and quarrying industries of the area. Today these provide a vein of rich historical interest and fascinating industrial archaeology. The mineral loop drew an ellipse through the heart of the Forest, linking with many other lines. This 7 mile route explores sections of the loop, generally on firm, wide paths with gentle gradients.

START Speech House Woodlands Car Park. SO 624125

DIRECTIONS The Speech House is midway between Coleford and Cinderford on the B4226. It was originally the verderer's court and is situated right in the centre of the Forest of Dean. It is now a hotel. The Woodlands parking area is on the north side of the road, a few hundred yards towards Cinderford.

PUBLIC TRANSPORT There is no regular bus service to the Speech House but route 31 (Gloucester – Cinderford – Coleford) runs along the A4136, passing through Brierley, 300 yards from point 4. This runs daily with a limited Sunday service.

I At the eastern end of the parking area, find a wooden post and follow the path indicated by the 'Gloucestershire Way' sign. This path slants gently down away from the road with woodland to the left and a clearing on the right. Go through a gate and TURN LEFT down the hill quite steeply on a forest track. When it comes to the bottom of the hill, at a T-junction, BEAR ROUND TO THE LEFT. Continue to follow the track as it descends more gently to a gate. You have now reached the family cycleway. This is also the track of the mineral loop line, marked by a sign 'White Gates'. *Just nearby an iron marker identifies the boundary of the Victorian 'Beechenhurst Inclosure'. Although there have long been rights of grazing in the Forest, laws passed in 1668 and 1808 permitted the fencing of certain 'inclosures' to pro-*

tect growing trees.

2 Once through the gate, TURN RIGHT to follow the track of the mineral loop line on a raised embankment. A little further on the track is decorated with twenty carved wooden sleepers. *This sculpture, entitled 'Iron Road' was created in 1986 as part of the 'Sculpture Trail'. The 4½ mile route starts from Beechenhurst Lodge and visits nearly 20 sculptures depicting the history and life of the Forest. For more details look at www.forestofdean-sculpture.org.uk.* At the end of the embankment rejoin the cycle trail at a junction of paths. Continue STRAIGHT AHEAD following the sign to Drybrook Road. *This is still the course of the mineral loop and you can see some relics of railway furniture such as old concrete fence posts.* The track climbs steadily on another embankment.

3 A little after the end of the embankment, there is a wooden gate in the fence on the right with a sign marked 'Sculpture Trail'. However, instead of going through this, climb up the short earthen path in the bank opposite, to the LEFT. You will find yourself on the course of another old line. *This place is Serridge Junction where the Lydbrook line joined the mineral loop. This line opened to traffic in 1875. If you look carefully, you will find one or two sleepers embedded in the earth.* TURN SHARP LEFT here and follow the grass and earthen course of the railway back through the woods, above the mineral loop. Soon you come to a more open area and join a hardcore forest track. CONTINUE STRAIGHT AHEAD as you join this, still following the line of the old Lydbrook railway round the shoulder of the hill. *After a while you pass above a grassy parking area known as*

28

Brierley (shop & bus stop)

④

'Speculation' after a colliery of the same name. Just past this the Lydbrook cycleway and track bed bear off to the left. But instead, KEEP ON THE MAIN TRACK straight ahead. _A little later, you can see some remains of Mireystock spoil heap now reclaimed by nature._ Further on cross a tarmac road.

4 If you divert left here along the tarmac road, a short walk will bring you to the main road at Brierley – _and a shop. There is also a bus stop._ Otherwise, cross the tarmac road and CONTINUE ALONG THE TRACK OPPOSITE, or rather, slightly to your right, past a barrier. After about half a mile, the track swings round to the right. _Hidden in the woods ahead of you are the remains of the Northern United Colliery, the last working underground coal mine in the Forest. It closed in 1965._ Climb to meet a tarmac lane. TURN SHARP RIGHT along this, over the brow of the hill and down the other side. At the bottom of the short hill, you come to a junction of tracks.

5 This is the site of Drybrook Road station. You have now rejoined the mineral loop at the junction of its branch to Cinderford. TURN LEFT to follow the cycleway towards Dilke Bridge. The track swings right to climb around industrial remains, with views of

Cinderford through the trees. It passes under a road near the Dilke Hospital. A quarter mile further on, the path veers RIGHT through a gate at Lightmoor sawmill.

6 Once through the gate, continue STRAIGHT AHEAD up the hill, ignoring the new course of the cycle way that turns left here. At the top of the hill, leave the track, which turns sharp left. Instead, BEAR RIGHT along a forest trail around a recently felled area. It soon curves left and comes to a wide junction of tracks. BEAR RIGHT and then maintain this direction, ignoring crossings and turnings. When the main track itself swings to the left, KEEP STRAIGHT AHEAD now on a wide footpath. This now veers gently to the right and slowly ascends. Pass through the arboretum and on to the road. The car park and starting point lies a few yards to the right.

**T**he Mineral Loop was part of the network of lines built by the Severn and Wye Railway in the nineteenth century to transport the mineral riches of Dean. It opened to traffic in 1872 and most of the old track bed is now used as a footpath or a cycle way. This walk follows much of its course. The Severn and Wye 'main line' ran on through Parkend to Lydney, then over a bridge to Sharpness on the eastern bank of the Severn. The 'Loop' was closed in various stages in the 1950s. A petrol tanker crashed into the Severn Railway Bridge in 1960, killing five people and demolishing two central spans. The railway never reopened and the bridge was taken down in 1970.

29

CANNOP, PARKEND & SPRUCE DRIVE

DESCRIPTION An interesting 7½ mile tour of the central Forest. The route takes advantage of the course of old railways and forest tracks, exploring some of the history and natural beauty of the mineral-rich woodlands. There are good tracks and gentle gradients.

START New Fancy car park. SO 627095. The walk could equally well be started from the Speech House (point **3**), Cannop (point **4**) or Parkend (point **5**).

DIRECTIONS New Fancy is just over a mile south of the Speech House, at a junction with the minor road between Parkend and Blakeney.

PUBLIC TRANSPORT Bus 727 from Parkend and Lydney serves the Barracks, at the road junction adjacent to New Fancy. This runs Mon-Sat only.

I Look for a cycleway marker at the lower end of the car park. Follow this out of the car park and descend RIGHT down a path to join a track. This soon leads to the main family cycleway through a gate, marked by a signpost. TURN LEFT here. Soon, at a crossing of tracks, the main route of the cycle way turns left and a branch to Mallard's Pike leads right (see **Walks 17** and **18**). This is actually the line of the 'mineral loop' (See **Walk 15** for more details of this industrial railway.) *The embankment is clearly evident here and you can spot pieces of extraneous railway archaeology such as old fence posts.* However, at this junction, cross over the course of this old line and continue STRAIGHT AHEAD, descending gradually to the bottom of the valley of Blackpool Brook. At the junction, KEEP LEFT on the well-made track and thankfully ignore the rather muddy route through the woods directly ahead. The track, now also a jogging course, soon crosses the brook and climbs to reach another junction.

2 At this point, leave the track as it turns right and instead TURN LEFT to follow a wide avenue known as Spruce Ride. *In a dip, pass the Speech House Lake on the left. The angling is private, but a path leads round the edge if you want to explore further.* At the end of the Ride, a gate leads into a parking area and then to the road, a short way south of the Speech House Hotel. *On your right is an entrance to the Speech House arboretum. There is a good variety of native species of trees here and also a trail for visually impaired people. Access is free at all times.*

3 TURN LEFT and follow the road. There is plenty of room on the unfenced verges to walk through the woods parallel to the road. Pass a special school on the right. About 200 yards after the school, and next to the 'SLOW' markings on the road, TURN RIGHT and cross a stile on to a forest road. The Gloucestershire Way footpath soon joins you. The way markers for this are a useful guide as far as point **4**. At a junction of paths, keep to the right as the track veers down hill. Later, at a T-junction, TURN LEFT. After a more level section you come to a crossing of tracks. Here TURN RIGHT, again following the footpath signs. You soon emerge at Cannop Wharf on the family cycle way and old mineral loop line. *The wharf here was built in the early nineteenth century as an interchange between the railway and tramway. A tramway ran up Bix Slade towards quarries at the top (See **Walk 14**). The pond was created by a dam, built in 1825 to power a water wheel further downstream at Parkend.*

4 TURN LEFT and follow the cycle way. Cross the road with care. *Notice the remains of the original railway course, which went under a bridge here.* The path skirts a yard with some industrial units and leads on to an access road. When this comes to a main road, carry STRAIGHT AHEAD on to an unmade road known as Crown Lane. Pass a recreation ground on the left and maintain this direction through some bollards and along the footpath and grass to join the road at the Fountain Inn.

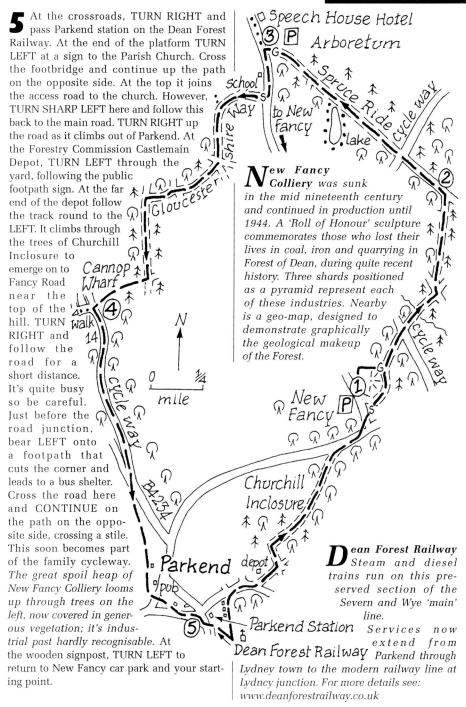

5 At the crossroads, TURN RIGHT and pass Parkend station on the Dean Forest Railway. At the end of the platform TURN LEFT at a sign to the Parish Church. Cross the footbridge and continue up the path on the opposite side. At the top it joins the access road to the church. However, TURN SHARP LEFT here and follow this back to the main road. TURN RIGHT up the road as it climbs out of Parkend. At the Forestry Commission Castlemain Depot, TURN LEFT through the yard, following the public footpath sign. At the far end of the depot follow the track round to the LEFT. It climbs through the trees of Churchill Inclosure to emerge on to Fancy Road near the top of the hill. TURN RIGHT and follow the road for a short distance. It's quite busy so be careful. Just before the road junction, bear LEFT onto a footpath that cuts the corner and leads to a bus shelter. Cross the road here and CONTINUE on the path on the opposite side, crossing a stile. This soon becomes part of the family cycleway. *The great spoil heap of New Fancy Colliery looms up through trees on the left, now covered in generous vegetation; it's industrial past hardly recognisable.* At the wooden signpost, TURN LEFT to return to New Fancy car park and your starting point.

New Fancy Colliery *was sunk in the mid nineteenth century and continued in production until 1944. A 'Roll of Honour' sculpture commemorates those who lost their lives in coal, iron and quarrying in Forest of Dean, during quite recent history. Three shards positioned as a pyramid represent each of these industries. Nearby is a geo-map, designed to demonstrate graphically the geological makeup of the Forest.*

Dean Forest Railway *Steam and diesel trains run on this preserved section of the Severn and Wye 'main' line. Services now extend from Parkend through Lydney town to the modern railway line at Lydney junction. For more details see:* www.deanforestrailway.co.uk

Map labels: Speech House Hotel · Arboretum · Spruce Ride · cycle way · school · Shire Way · to New Fancy · lake · Gloucester · Cannop Wharf · walk 14 · cycle way · New Fancy · Churchill Inclosure · Parkend · pub · depot · Parkend Station · Dean Forest Railway · mile · N

AWRE'S GLOW & STAPLE EDGE

DESCRIPTION The climb up Staple Edge is well graded and provides some great views across the Forest. You may also be lucky enough to see wild boar, deer and a wide variety of bird life on this quiet but accessible route. Almost the whole circuit is on good tracks and mo ' is easily navigable by wheelchairs or pushchairs but, at 6 miles, it is quite a long walk, and there is one section right at the end NOT suitable for wheels.

START Mallard's Pike – Forestry Commission car park and picnic area. SO 637092. Parking charge. There are toilets here. There is usually a refreshment van during the most popular holiday periods.

DIRECTIONS The entrance to Mallard's Pike is about 1½ miles east of Parkend on the minor road to Blakeney.

PUBLIC TRANSPORT Bus 727 from Parkend – Lydney serves the Barracks (a road junction ¼ mile west of Mallard's Pike) Mon-Sat only.

I Facing the lake, and with your back to the toilet block, TURN RIGHT to follow the path around the lake. At the end of the lake TURN LEFT across a footbridge over the outflow and continue right around the lake on the shore path. At the end of the path, you come to a wide track between the two lakes. FOLLOW THE TRACK RIGHT. It almost immediately curves back to the left and follows a line of electricity poles through a clearing in the forest. *This long clearing through the Forest is known as Awre's Glow. On a sunny day it is a good site for butterflies. When researching this route, I suddenly came to a halt when two small furry creatures squealed across the track in front of me. I soon realised there were another half dozen specimens and two rather larger adult wild boars nearby. Boars were released in Dean in the autumn of 2004. Since then they have become more widespread and their activities have been a source of heated con-*

troversy. Although an interesting spectacle, they can cause damage. As with any animals with young, the best advice is to back off and give them a clear space. They seemed to take little interest in me! Nearly 1½ miles after Mallard's Pike, the wide track ends at a T-junction.

2 At the junction, TURN RIGHT and climb a little more steeply to another T-junction. This time, TURN SHARP LEFT. The track ascends gently to a brow and then begins to lose height. Soon after the descent begins, you come to a major intersection.

3 TAKE THE RIGHT HAND FORK and follow this as it curves to the right, around the end of the Staple Edge ridge. You now begin to climb quite steeply. There are views through the trees into the Soudley valley below you to the left. Once the track levels out, it follows a clearing near the crest of the ridge. At a junction of paths, you may be able to see Staple-edge bungalows through the trees to your right, but our track CURVES LEFT and drops gently to a gate next to a small pond.

4 PASS THROUGH THE GATE and continue along the forest track, ignoring the footpath forking to the left. (Just over 50 yards past this gate a small grass footpath leads RIGHT gently down through the trees to rejoin the main track at Point **5**. It is easy to miss the turning, so watch out for it carefully if you want to take this short cut.) The main route continues along the track and soon begins to lose height, increasingly rapidly. It winds down to reach a junction of tracks, marked by a wooden waymark on the left. TURN SHARP RIGHT here and contour back round the ridge.

5 The track sweeps left (where the short cut rejoins us), and you cross a small stream. *The route traverses the southern side of Staple Edge Wood and views open out across the Forest towards Yorkley.* The track begins to descend as it rounds the shoulder of the hill. Towards the bottom of the slope, you come to a junction. Here the main track DOUBLES BACK LEFT to regain a southerly direction. Soon a short path leads RIGHT by a marker post down to rejoin the lakeside path. (This short section is the one awkward place for wheels on the main route – though you could avoid it by continuing on the track towards the road and turning back to the car park further on.) Once at the lake, TURN LEFT to follow the path back to the start.

*T**he present lakes** at Mallard's 'ike are a relatively recent feature. Unusually, the original purpose was not industrial but recreational. The two linked ponds were laid out in the 1970s. Although you may find mallards (and other water birds) here, the name does not derive from either birds or fish. The 'pike' refers to a turnpike a short way from the spot. Maller was the name of its occupant until about 50 years ago. Today, this is a picturesque and popular spot in the heart of the Forest. It is the start of a waymarked jogging course and is home to a rope activity centre. The path round the lakes provides an accessible wheelchair or push-chair route.*

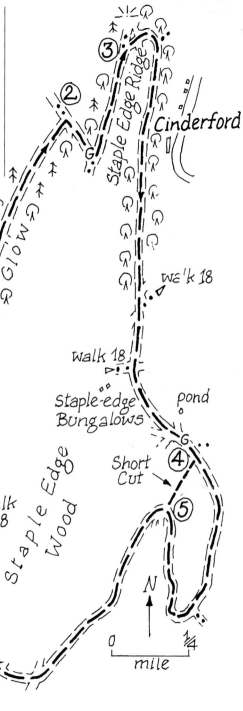

33

STAPLE EDGE, SOUDLEY VALLEY & WENCHFORD

DESCRIPTION A 6½-mile tour of the eastern fringes of the Forest. A traverse of the wooded Staple Edge escarpment is followed by an exploration of the Soudley valley along the track of an old railway. The return route climbs through Blakeneyhill Wood before dropping down to Wenchford picnic site. The walk is mostly along good tracks but there are some forest footpaths, which can be damp in wet weather.

START Mallard's Pike – Forestry Commission car park and picnic area. SO 637092. Parking charge. There are toilets here. There is often a refreshment van during the most popular holiday periods.

DIRECTIONS The entrance to Mallard's Pike is about 1½ miles east of Parkend on the minor road to Blakeney.

PUBLIC TRANSPORT Route 727 Parkend – Lydney serves the Barracks (a road junction ¼ mile west of Mallard's Pike) Mon-Sat only.

1 Facing the lake, and with your back to the toilet block, TURN RIGHT to follow the path around the lake. At the end of the lake TURN LEFT across a footbridge over the outflow. A few yards further, leave the perimeter path RIGHT at a sign for 'Wenchford link'. Follow the arrow through the trees and come to a gravel road. TURN LEFT here and follow the road until it comes to a sharp right hand turn. Instead of following this, keep STRAIGHT ON along a forest track. In about 400 yards a post indicates a forest path leaving the track. TURN RIGHT here and follow the path diagonally uphill through the trees. At the top of the steepest section, BEAR LEFT onto another track, following the yellow arrow. Soon the track arrives at a collection of buildings surrounded by a hedge. *These are known as Staple-edge Bungalows.*

2 TURN LEFT on to the broad track round the houses. By the last house, BEAR RIGHT to follow a footpath marked by a yellow arrow. After a short distance come to a crossing with a major gravel track. TURN LEFT, ignoring the footpath straight ahead. After about 300 yards, watch out for a track to the RIGHT diving down the hill between some oak trees. There is no sign so watch carefully. (There is a second right turning just a few yards further on, but our route follows the FIRST of the pair.) A good wide path leads down the hill, soon passing some old spoil heaps, and descending steadily to the main road along the Soudley valley.

3 Cross the road with great care and find a small footpath directly opposite. Follow this a short distance downhill to the bottom of the valley and TURN RIGHT along a trail. *The local parish council built this as a Millennium project on the bed of the Soudley Valley railway. The railway was opened in 1854 and closed in 1967. The track is now also part of a geological trail around Soudley. Further down the track pause at the site of Soudley furnace, built under the authority of King James I in 1613. The furnace supplied shot to the royalists in the English Civil War, during which Charles I besieged nearby Gloucester. A sculpture depicts the Forest of Dean 'hod boys', who hauled coal from the face to the pit ponies deep underground. There is also a simple memorial stone to the 5,000 Forest sheep culled during the 2001 Foot and Mouth outbreak.* Continue until the track meets the road. TURN RIGHT for a few yards and then take the FIRST LEFT along Lower Road. At the end of the road, TURN RIGHT over a bridge towards the village hall. Immediately after the bridge, but before the hall, TURN LEFT along a grassy track. Follow this, with the river on your left. It comes to a clearing by a small pumping station.

4 TURN RIGHT here to follow an earthen footpath climbing into the woods up the right hand side of a small valley. It goes through a wooden gap. Carry straight on in this direction, crossing another track, until you arrive at a surfaced lane. CROSS

THE LANE and continue along a Forestry Commission gravel road marked 'Private access. No entry to unauthorised vehicles.' Walk through mature mixed woodland on a pleasant track. In just over half a mile, come to a clearing and a complex junction of tracks next to some houses. Keep STRAIGHT AHEAD joining a major gravel track, following this for about 200 yards. It ends at a turning area by Blakeney Hill Lodge.

5 LEAVE THE TRACK HERE, BEARING RIGHT along a grassy path following the line of the electricity poles. In a few yards arrive at a large pylon. A long, wide clearing lies ahead, followed by the electricity lines. However, at the pylon, our route BEARS DOWN RIGHT into the trees on a good, if damp, path. In a while, at a junction, continue straight ahead on a broad gravel track along a wide avenue of oak trees. Where the track bears left, choose a smaller path BEARING RIGHT directly down to Wenchford car park and picnic site. There are toilets here.

6 Just in front of the toilet block, find a green-topped post indicating the Blackpool Brook Trail. Follow the posts along the bottom of the valley, next to the brook through the picnic area. When this rejoins the main track, continue across on the other side, following a white arrow marking the route towards Mallard's Pike. Continue on this path, which may also be used by cycles, so take care. *On your left you can see the embankment of the old Forest of Dean Central railway, which originally connected Howbeach Colliery, near Mallard's Pike*

to the main Gloucester – Cardiff line at Awre Junction. *This section closed in 1942.* When you come to a road, CROSS IT. Continue on the track on the opposite side, indicated by a white arrow. This climbs steadily through the woods before curving to the right and descending towards Mallard's Pike. At the bottom, there is a right turn and shortly afterwards a sign points LEFT down to the lake. Continue around the perimeter path to the starting point.

The Wye Valley

BLAIZE BAILEY & SOUDLEY PONDS

DESCRIPTION An excellent panorama of the Severn's great horseshoe bend from one of the Forest's most spectacular viewpoints. This is the prize for a relatively modest climb on a good track. The return route offers the opportunity to visit the Dean Heritage Centre to explore the history and culture of the Forest. A gentle lake side stroll rounds off the walk. At 4 miles, this is a short outing, but full of interest.

START Soudley Ponds Forestry car park. SO 663116

DIRECTIONS The car park is less than a mile north of Soudley on a minor road towards Littledean. This leaves the unclassified Cinderford to Blakeney road in Soudley village, close to the Dean Heritage Centre.

PUBLIC TRANSPORT Use bus 717 and start at point **5**. This route runs between Lydney and Cinderford, passing the Dean Heritage Centre and Soudley village. The service is approximately hourly on weekdays.

1 From the car park, pass the forest barrier and take the LEFT of the two forestry roads that climb the hill. The track slants diagonally up the hillside. Towards the top the track veers to the RIGHT as it passes a house a little way to the left. It gains the crest of the ridge and soon comes to a triangular junction. BEAR LEFT here and continue for about 100 yards to Blaize Bailey viewpoint.

2 *The viewpoint is right on the eastern fringe of the Forest of Dean plateau. There is a spectacular panorama of the great horseshoe bend in the River Severn, and beyond it to the Cotswold escarpment and the city of Gloucester.* Return to the triangular junction and TURN SHARP LEFT to continue along the ridge on a fine, wide forestry track. Further along there are more views through the trees down to the Severn estuary.

3 About a mile from Blaize Bailey, as you begin to descend, the track SWINGS SHARPLY TO THE RIGHT. Ignore the footpath post pointing straight ahead and follow this main track. This contours around the other side of the hill, offering westward views into the Soudley valley.

4 After about ¼ mile, at point **4**, you find a clear, but less well used, track slanting down the hillside and crossing the forestry road. It is marked with posts showing a 'no horse riding' logo. BEAR LEFT down this grassy track. It soon becomes a path, but is clear and obvious. Keep descending until you meet the main road, passing above the Dean Heritage Centre.

5 If you want to visit the museum, go through the gate and TURN LEFT along the road for a few yards (see details below). Otherwise, TURN RIGHT and follow the path along the side of the lake. This all-ability access route passes a series of small lakes (Soudley Ponds) and marshy areas. It is maintained as a nature reserve. It brings you back to the car park.

The Dean Heritage Centre is the museum of the Forest. Five galleries explore the geology, landscape, history and industry of this unique area. These use personal memories and recollections, as well as reconstructions and exhibits, so it is very much a living testimony to foresters past and present. Outside there is a reconstructed forester's cottage, a 'free' mine and a charcoal burner's camp. A comprehensive shop and café help to make this a great place to visit. Admission charge. For more information visit www. deanheritagemuseum.com.

The Severn has the second highest tidal range in the world. The estuary also becomes both narrow and shallow quickly. So as the tidal waters flood upstream they are funnelled into a natural wave or 'bore', a spectacular natural phenomenon. Bores are most likely to occur at the highest (spring) tides which happen every lunar cycle. Forecast times, and other information and advice, are available from: www.environment-agency.gov.uk/regions/ midlands. Needless to say, the estuary is a dangerous place and the bore should always be viewed from a safe location and with due courtesy for others. Many would say that the sound of the approaching wave is as impressive as its height or visual impact.

An alternative easy route for all abilities

Good paths allow a circumnavigation of Soudley Ponds, around a mile in length. From the start follow the firm track south. This is suitable for wheelchairs and pushchairs and leads directly to point 5 on the main walk. From here it is a short distance along the road to Dean Heritage Centre. To vary the return, a clear footpath follows the far side back to the car park, though this is not suitable for wheels.

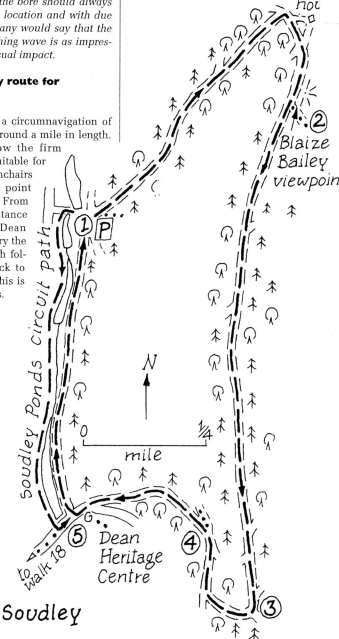

WALK 20

MAY HILL

DESCRIPTION Although less than a thousand feet high, May Hill is a distinctive landmark for many miles around, due to the characteristic clump of trees capping its summit. The top of the hill offers extensive views from a captivating dome of heath land. This circuit from Longhope is 4½ miles.

START Longhope Post Office,. SO 688189.

DIRECTIONS Longhope is just off the A4136 Gloucester – Monmouth road. The Post Office is a short way along the road through the village towards Lea and Ross. There is no car park but there is room for roadside parking at a number of places in the village.

PUBLIC TRANSPORT There is a regular daily service on route 24 Gloucester – Mitcheldean – Ruardean, including limited Sunday provision.

Between the Post Office and village shop, find a side road called Station Lane and follow this uphill out of the village. Cross the remains of the old railway line, still marked by a level crossing gate at the side. *This was the Hereford, Ross and Gloucester railway, originally opened in the 1850s. This direct link between the two cathedral cities was severed in the Beeching cuts during the 1960s, since when the rail route has involved a circuitous journey through Newport.* After the last house the lane gives way to a rutted track which keeps climbing through the trees. At the brow of the hill, keep straight ahead at a junction of paths and then descend between fields towards the A40 main road. Less than 100 yards before you come to the road, where the lane bends to the left, a right of way leaves the lane to cross the field on the right diagonally to a gate. There is no sign from the lane, but using this avoids a short but nasty stretch of footpath-less A40.

2 Cross the main road with due diligence as it is busy and visibility is limited. Follow the footpath on the opposite side, through a gate. Almost immediately, TURN RIGHT in front of a building and follow the right of way across a patch of rough grass towards a light yellow coloured house. The path goes through a gap at the right of this house and reaches a lane. KEEP STRAIGHT AHEAD and follow the road for about 300 yards until a cross roads. TURN LEFT following a sign for Yarleton Lane. After a short distance, TURN RIGHT to follow a bridleway which ascends between scattered houses. After the last dwelling, it reverts to a green lane winding up the hill. When you come to a lane, TURN LEFT and then shortly arrive at a junction of tracks next to a water tank. TURN LEFT, following the Gloucestershire Way sign along a good track. After a gate this leads on to open heath land, under the stewardship of the National Trust. Continue to the top of May Hill, which is crowned by a copse of trees and a trig point.

3 *The clump is a landmark for many miles and identifies this modest but distinctive elevation. There is a correspondingly extensive panorama from May Hill west to the Black Mountains; east to the Cotswold escarpment; and south across the Forest of Dean and the Severn estuary. This is a great place to sit and ponder for a while. The clump dates back many years. There is a story that Prince Rupert and some cavaliers sheltered here during the Siege of Gloucester in the English Civil War. The trees were augmented to celebrate both the Golden Jubilee of Queen Victoria (1887) and the Silver Jubilee of Queen Elizabeth (1977).* At the top of the hill TURN LEFT past the trig point to find a way marker at the top of a path leading west down hill. *The post identifies the route as the Gloucestershire Way and the Wysis Way.* Follow this broad grassy descent between gorse bushes to a gate. From here steps lead down through woodland to a lane at the bottom. TURN LEFT for a few yards before TURNING RIGHT across a stile to continue on the Gloucestershire Way. The way now leads down several fields and then weaves through a patch of light woodland before descending to a small lane. TURN LEFT along this narrow lane. When it joins another lane TURN LEFT once more. Follow this for about 150 yards until just before an old railway arch. BEAR LEFT on to a public footpath through a kissing gate. Follow the path across a field, over the embankment of the former railway, across a footbridge and then over another field to the main road.

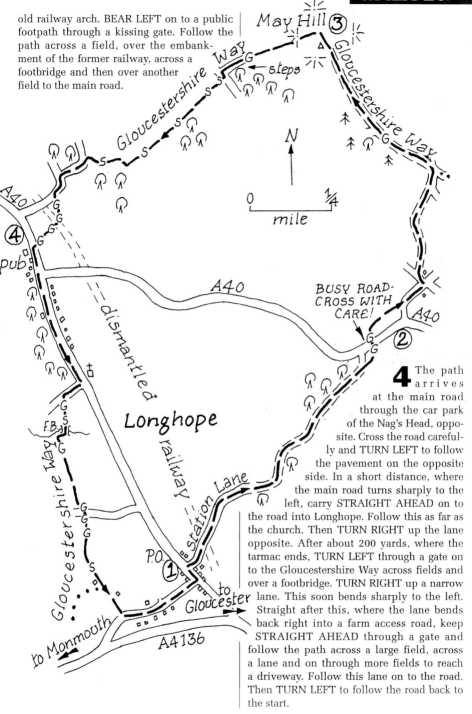

4 The path arrives at the main road through the car park of the Nag's Head, opposite. Cross the road carefully and TURN LEFT to follow the pavement on the opposite side. In a short distance, where the main road turns sharply to the left, carry STRAIGHT AHEAD on to the road into Longhope. Follow this as far as the church. Then TURN RIGHT up the lane opposite. After about 200 yards, where the tarmac ends, TURN LEFT through a gate on to the Gloucestershire Way across fields and over a footbridge. TURN RIGHT up a narrow lane. This soon bends sharply to the left. Straight after this, where the lane bends back right into a farm access road, keep STRAIGHT AHEAD through a gate and follow the path across a large field, across a lane and on through more fields to reach a driveway. Follow this lane on to the road. Then TURN LEFT to follow the road back to the start.

General advice

Walks in this book vary from 2 to 10 miles. Some are relatively gentle strolls and others are more serious excursions. This is not a remote area. Even in the depths of the Forest of Dean, you will never be far from a road or human habitation. Nevertheless, it is sensible to be prepared. Tracks can be muddy and there are steep and slippery sections on some walks, so a good pair of boots is essential. Take spare clothing, waterproofs and a first aid kit.

In forested areas marked tracks may have disappeared or become overgrown, so be alert for turnings and use contours and other mapping features, or even a compass or GPS, to help your navigation.

Details of access by public transport have been included at the start of each walk. The nearest railway stations are Chepstow and Lydney. There are regular bus services through many parts of the area. For details of public transport contact:

Traveline (www.traveline.org.uk or 0871 200 22 33).

Alternatively you can access bus timetables at:

www.gloucestershire.gov.uk

www.monmouthshire.gov.uk

www.herefordshire.gov.uk

KEY TO THE MAPS

- Walk route and direction
- Main road
- Minor road
- Path
- River/stream
- Woods
- Railway
- **G** Gate
- **S** Stile
- View
- **P** Parking

THE COUNTRYSIDE CODE

- Be safe – plan ahead and follow any signs
- Leave gates and property as you find them
- Protect plants and animals, and take your litter home
- Keep dogs under close control
- Consider other people

Open Access

Some routes cross areas of land where walkers have the legal right of access under The CRoW Act 2000 introduced in May 2005. Access can be subject to restrictions and closure for land management or safety reasons for up to 28 days a year. Details from www.naturalresourceswales.gov.uk or www.naturalengland.gov.uk.

Published by
Kittiwake
3 Glantwymyn Village Workshops, Glantwymyn, Machynlleth, Montgomeryshire SY20 8LY

© Text & map research: Alastair Ross 2010
© Maps (from ooc refs) & illustrations: Kittiwake 2010
Drawings by Morag Perrott

Cover photos: *Main* – The Wye Valley from Symond's Yat. *Inset* – Tintern Abbey. *David Perrott*

Care has been taken to be accurate. However neither the author nor the publisher can accept responsibility for any errors which may appear, or their consequences. If you are in any doubt about access, check before you proceed.

Printed byMixam, UK.

ISBN: **978 1902302 77 5**